Frank Siller

The Song of Manitoba

And other Poems

Frank Siller

The Song of Manitoba
And other Poems

ISBN/EAN: 9783337181932

Printed in Europe, USA, Canada, Australia, Japan

Cover: Foto ©Thomas Meinert / pixelio.de

More available books at **www.hansebooks.com**

THE SONG OF MANITOBA

AND OTHER

POEMS

BY

FRANK SILLER.

~~~~~

T. S. GRAY COMPANY,
MILWAUKEE.
1888.

DEDICATION.

Beside our faith there is no power
   To guide and comfort us, so strong,
In joy and in life's saddest hour,
   As that of poetry and song.

Let therefore all, whom God has granted
   The gift of song, attune their harp;
Their melodies are ever wanted—
   Be they in minor keys or sharp—

Not only by the few elected,
   Who take them as they quaff their wine,
But by the lowly, the neglected,
   To whom they are a gift Divine.

Aye, even to the very singer
   They often consolation gave,
And there are hearts wherein they linger
   And solace them e'en to the grave!—

INDEX.

POEMS TRANSLATED.

INDEX—Continued.

VI.

INDEX—Continued.

THE SONG OF MANITOBA.

(Based on an Indian tradition from which the name Manitoba originated.)

Sound once more, thou harp of ages, the north
    wind tune thy strings,
To that gale which from the prairies nature's
    freshest fragrance brings,

Rich with scent of meads and wildwoods, laden,
    too, with ancient lays,
Strange old legends and traditions of the far-off
    Indian days.

*   *   *

Midway from where Mississippi's turbid waters
    gulfward flow,
To the sea of icy mountains, glistening in the mid-
    night glow—

Midway from where swift St. Lawrence past the
    "Thousand Islands" sweeps,
To where grand Columbia river o'er the coast-
    range madly leaps—

Dwelt the powerful Ojibways on their glorious
    hunting ground,
Where dense forests, moors and meadows Mani-
    toba lake surround.

Manitoba lake was known to Indian nations far
    and wide,
And, to worship Manitou, they often wandered to
    its tide.

In the lake there was an island with dense forest
    overgrown,
From whose shore was often heard what they
    believed the solemn tone

Of the voice of Manitou, thus Manitoba was its
    name,
Manitoba—Speaking God—and to the lake the
    people came

From the distant Athabaska, from the great
　　Saskatchewan,
From the limpid lake Itaska, from the waters of
　　Wakan,*

Where, through subterranean caverns, rose the
　　wild Assiniboin,†
With their warriors, in the hunt, the brave Dakotah
　　tribes to join.

Here they met, and here they worshipped God from
　　immemorial time,
Listening, with their hearts devout, to Manitoba's
　　wondrous chime.

Sacred was the island held; the boldest even of the
　　braves
Dared not touch its shore, though oft they sailed
　　o'er Manitoba's waves.

'Twas a hazy dreamy morn; the summer's hunt
　　was fairly done,
And the buffalo and deer-meat drying in the
　　autumn sun;

Crops of wild rice had been gathered by the
　　squaws for winter store,
And the youths, to pass the time, were shooting
　　fish along the shore.

Groups of men were idly lounging in the shade of
    elm and oak,
Blowing, from their red stone pipes, into the air
    the curling smoke—

When, oh wonder, o'er the lake, there came a large
    and winged canoe,
Which, with wind that came from sunrise, to the
    Indian village flew.

Pale-faced, black-robed men were in it; with them
    came an Indian guide,
Who had led them all the way to Manitoba's sacred
    tide.

Kindly were they all received, and far and wide
    the news was sent,
That beside the Indian's wigwam pale-faced men
    had pitched their tent.

Many chiefs and braves arrived, to see the white
    men, who had come
From the rising sun, to visit the Ojibway's happy
    home.

One day, as they were assembled on the fresh and
    fragrant sod,
And the white men tried to tell the Indians some-
    thing of their God,

4

Lo! there came the solemn music from the Island's
    distant shore;
Wondering stood the whites—such sounds as these
    they ne'er had heard before.

But the Indians toward the island bent their heads
    in silent awe,
And in prayer. This, with amazement ill-con-
    cealed, the white men saw.

Then their Indian guide they questioned: "Whence
    these sounds and why this prayer?"
He said, pointing to the island: "Manitou is speak-
    ing there!"

When the Indians' prayers were ended, spoke the
    black-robed pale-face chief,
And, his words interpreting, the Indian guide gave
    thus in brief:

"Friends! a strange illusion governs your devo-
    tion and your prayer,
If you faithfully believe, that Manitou is speaking
    there:

"Let us go to yonder island, let us search it o'er
    and o'er,
And we certainly will find what makes this music
    on the shore."

Of the Indians none would venture, save Venasco,
    old and gray,
Who, by eloquence and wisdom, the united tribes
    could sway.

Even he, with secret tremor, now the sacred isle
    approached,
For he indistinctly felt that he on hallowed
    ground encroached.

When they reached the island's shore, they found
    a beach of solid stone,
Which, when beaten with its fragments, gave a
    ringing, chime-like tone.

When the northwind raised the surf, which o'er
    this beach the pebbles rolled,
Sounds went forth across the lake, as if some dis-
    tant bells were tolled.

Old Venasco stood in silence, with his eyes cast to
    the ground,
As he watched the rolling pebbles, as he listened
    to the sound.

But the pale-face chief, approaching, said to him,
    in gentle tone:
"With what here thine eyes behold, thy faith in
    Manitou is gone?

"Let it go, for I will tell thee and thy people of *the*
    God,
Who to mankind promised heaven and sealed the
    promise with his blood."

And he told Venasco much about the Savior, who
    had come
To the earth to show its children how to reach
    their heavenly home.

And he told them how He lived; how, bleeding on
    the cross, He died,
That the faith in Him may save all human beings
    far and wide.

When the white man ceased to speak, the Indian
    proudly waved his hand,
Saying: "Friend! one lesson only can I thus far
    understand.

"When we thought that from this island Manito-
    ba's voice was heard
Any more than he speaks elsewhere to humanity,
    we erred.

"But thou errest, if thou thinkest that I've lost
    my living faith;
Faith in Manitou can leave me only with my dying
    breath.

"He can speak to all his people best in nature's
    voice, and hence
Needs no pale-faced men to tell us how to do him
    reverence.

"Here he speaks through waves and pebbles, roll-
    ing on the sounding stone,
Elsewhere may his voice be heard in roaring gales
    and thunder-tone.

"Mild appear his words when spoken through the
    pine trees, straight and tall,
Loud and angry seems their sound at Mississippi
    waterfall.

"Seek not to disturb our faith, since nothing bet-
    ter thou canst give,
For my people, like myself, will still in Manitou
    believe!"

But the pale-faced men, returning, told the guide
    how they had found,
That the waves and pebbles caused on yonder isle
    the chime-like sound.

Thus the news among the people spread like wild-
    fire far and near,
Filling them with dark misgivings, and their
    hearts with doubt and fear.

But Venasco called a council of the chieftains, wise
    and bold,
And, what he had seen and heard on yonder isle,
    he plainly told.

Also told, what he had answered; this the older
    chiefs approved:
But the young men and the squaws were by the
    white men's stories moved.

Yet in this they all united, that a meeting they
    would hold,
When both sides should to the nations proof of
    their belief unfold.

This was done; the pale-face chief read, from his
    gold-clasped sacred book,
Wondertales, which many an Indian's heart and
    fancy captive took.

Said, that those, who would believe what in this
    sacred book he found,
Surely would, when leaving life, go to the happy
    hunting ground;

While the souls of those who held to Manitoba's
    foolish faith,
Would be burned in fire more fierce, than burning
    forests—after death.

9

Waen the black-robed chief had ended, old Venasco
    took his stand
'Neath a giant oak, and toward the setting sun he
    stretched his hand.

But his face was turned toward midnight with a
    strange and distant gaze,
Seemingly he tried to fathom Manitoba's hidden
    ways.

Then he spoke: "Great light of heaven, oh! glori-
    ous sun, thou sinkest deep
'Neath the land that we can see, and with thee all
    things go to sleep.

" But to-morrow thou returnest, waking all to life
    and light—
And ye stars, obscured by day, but keeping watch
    throughout the night;

"All ye glorious lights were placed by Manitou's,
    the master's, hand.
Who has also made the prairies, forests, rivers, sea
    and land!"

Then Venasco, toward his people turning, said:
    " In nature's way
Ye must walk and worship Him, then will ye never
    go astray.

"What he is and how to love Him, He has writ in
    every heart,
And we need no pale-faced men, from books such
    knowledge to impart!"

Up toward heaven Venasco raised his face and
    hands in fervent prayer:
"Master!" spoke he, "if I'm wrong, oh! end my
    life, do not forbear;

"Let thy fiercest flash descend from yonder cloud-
    roll, dark and bleak;
But if truth I told, Great Spirit, Manitou—atoba—
    speak!"‡

Barely had these words he uttered, when a livid
    lightning flash
Rent the oak from top to root and smote it down
    with fearful crash;

Loud reverberating thunder rolled o'er lake and
    sloping sod,
And its echoes seemed to murmer "Daring mortal!
    tempt not God!"

In a trance Venasco stood, his face upturned, his
    hands upheld,
While a sudden northern gale the dark and threat-
    ening clouds dispelled.

11

Rays of light illumed the sky, the boreal aurora
    shone;
From the distant island sounded solemnly the
    well-known tone.

All the Indians bowed their heads and worshiped
    Manitoba's might.
And, before the dawn of day, the black-robed
    white men took their flight.

Many years have passed, the Indians die, their
    place the white men fill,
Where once the Ojibway hunted, white men now
    rich wheat fields till.

Ah, the savage hunter could not be induced to
    wield the plough,
Nor that dusky son of nature made before the cross
    to bow.

But the mighty wheel of progress, like the planet
    onward bound,
Crushes all such obstacles, with force resistless, to
    the ground.

Now on Manitoba lake a Christian population
    dwells,
Called to church and to the schoolhouse by the
    voice of metal bells.

Yet the worship of Venasco and the ancient Indian time,
Still is often called to mind by Manitoba's wondrous chime.

---

*Wakan, or Minne-Wakan, in English "Devil's Lake."

†"Rose, the wild Assiniboin." The old traditions of that Indian tribe is that they came from the interior of the earth through caverns still existing near Devil's lake.

‡"Maniton-atoba." The Assiniboin "watum," imperative "watumwa," by the Ojibway pronounced more like "atoba," means in English to whisper loudly or to speak; hence the name Manitoba means "the whispering great spirit," or "the speaking Deity."

THE PETRIFIED FOREST.*

A VISION.

The Rocky Mountain summits
  Hold, high in a cliff-bound bed,
A lake of crystal clearness,
  By springs from snow-peaks fed.

Its rocky shores are lonely,
  Devoid of beast or bird,
And in the distance only
  The wood-dove's call is heard.

In a glen on the stony margin
  A small canoe I spied,
And, clambering down, soon floated
  Upon the crystal tide;

And looking into the water
  Unruffled by the breeze,
I saw far down beneath me
  The tops of mighty trees.

---

* A few miles from Georgetown, Colorado, 10,400 feet above the ocean level, lies "Green Lake." Far beneath its surface in clear weather the tree-tops of a petrified forest can be seen and at great depth the mountain trout distinguished swimming among the branches.

Those trees were no reflection,
  I looked with eager care,
And pondered o'er the question:
  "How came that forest there?"

And while absorbed in thinking,
  My heavy eyelids closed,
And soon the lonely boatman
  In slumber deep reposed.

Canoe and water vanished
  Before my dreaming eyes,
While a sylph-like swan descended
  From the bright and cloudless skies.

She seemed to call me downward,
  Alighting 'neath a tree,
And in gentle tones related
  This wonder-tale to me:

"'Tis many a thousand years, man,
  Since here, where now we rest,
There stood a thrifty forest,
  With flowers and verdure blest.

"With singing birds this valley
  In those days did abound,
And from its hidden rock-glens
  Was heard the echo's sound.

"A wizard o'er this region
  His mighty scepter swayed,
And held here as a captive
  A young and lovely maid.

"Far from the Aztec country
  The enchanter had beguiled
The maid to this lone valley—
  She was a king's own child.

"Her heart was gay and happy,
  She loved the fragrant flowers,
She vied with the birds in singing,
  And played with the echo for hours.

"Deep in the midst of the forest
  A well-spring, cold and clear,
Gushed from the rocks; a grotto
  Of stone and moss stood near;

"Around it ferns and flowers;
  A shady, lonely place;
Here dwelt the forest spirit,
  Young, faun-like, full of grace.

"The wizard oft in friendship
  Had shared this youth's kind board—
One delved for gold and silver,
  In dreams the other soared.

16

"The youth had met the maiden;
  She soon his heart possessed,
Her own to him she promised,
  Half serious, half in jest.

"The wizard overheard them;
  He wished her for his wife,
And from that moment plotted
  Against his rival's life.

"In neither look nor language
  His purpose he betrayed,
But, 'neath the ground descending.
  His plan he deeply laid.

"He undermined with his goblins
  The forest's breadth and length,
And placed in the excavations
  Earth poisons of virulent strength.

"Ah then the branches withered,
  To stone the forest turned,
Birds perished, wild flowers shriveled
  As though they had been burned.

"The thoughtless, terrified maiden
  Accepted the wizard's hand,
And, heartsick, entered with him
  His subterranean land

17

4

"That glistened with gold and silver
  And gems of every kind;
They pleased her not, she could not,
  In riches, comfort find.

"A friendly elf in secret,
  Had whispered in her ear,
What petrified the forest,—
  Then naught could hold her here.

"A wild desire possessed her
  To see the light of day,
And, be it life's last duty,
  Few words to her friend to say.

"Through devious secret caverns
  The elf his mistress led,
But, ah, the wily wizard,
  Unseen, behind them sped.

"On reaching the spirit's grotto,
  Bowed o'er the spring she beheld
His wasted form, and in anguish
  Beside her friend she knelt.

"'Forgive,' she cried, 'forgive me,
  My selfish, faithless course;
My heart, that ever loved thee,
  Is stung with deep remorse!'

18

"She saw him quiver and tremble,
  The color left his face;
She feared for his life—and that moment
  She held him in tender embrace.

"To stone her touch had turned him;
  She rose with a piercing cry,
And anguished, yet defiant,
  She met the wizard's eye.

"'Thou dids't this,' cried she trembling,
  'Thou feared and hated man!'
But he, in jealous frenzy,
  Pronounced his sorcerer's ban:

"'An image of stone thy lover,
  A lone swan thou shalt be!'
Thus cried the wizard raging,
  Then up to the peaks rushed he.

"With might he shook the mountains,
  'Mid crashing thunder-sound
The cliffs fell, he fell with them,
  'Neath them his grave he found.

"The cliffs and boulders falling,
  Had formed a wall below,
Which closed the gorge of the valley,
  And checked its water-flow.

"And from the snowy summits
    Descended floods of tears,
They have submerged the forest
    For many a thousand years.

"Now give to the world, kind mortal,
    This song at the swan's request,
Then shall the spell be broken,
    And a poor soul be at rest."

Thus had the swan-sylph spoken,
    I dreamily opened my eyes,
And saw from the limpid water
    A single swan arise.

Wild swans are wont to migrate
    In pairs—alone was she—
O could, perchance, this lone-swan
    That Aztec maiden be?

Impossible! thought I, awaking.
    Afloat in my frail little bark,
While far o'er the lake the snow-peaks
    Cast shadows, chill and dark.

And I gazed deep down through the water—
    There was less light from above,
And the petrified forest appeared now
As the grave of friendship and love.

Ah, he to whom love was unfaithful,
  Who can trust to friendship no more,
Resembles that forest, a demon
  Has poisoned his heart to the core.

No flower sheds there its fragrance,
  No bird sings there its song,
But deep 'mong the paralyzed branches
  Dives coldly the fishes mute throng.

And even to kind consolations
  Sweet voice—no echo replies;
But at night from the depth are arising
  Low moans and sobs and sighs.

MANITOU SPRINGS.

[Colorado.]

The beautiful village of Manitou
  In a wonderful valley lies hidden,
And if you seek it, it offers you
  The treasures of nature unbidden.

Though its sentinel guardsmen, the grand
    Pike's Peak
  Before you reach it may greet you
With his snowy head and his face so bleak,
  He never advances to meet you.

21

Yet down in the valley, not far from his feet,
  With a quaint little fence for protection,
Three urns are placed in the village street,
  Whose contents are almost perfection.

These urns are carved out of granite strong
  And from them small streamlets are running;
Their liquid was mixed for the health-seeking
    throng
  By Nature's most consummate cunning.

It rises and bubbles like sparkling champagne,
  No crystal is purer and lighter,
It quenches the thirst, it alleviates pain,
  And makes you feel stronger and brighter.

With thousandfold treasures of silver and gold
  Colorado may becken the masses;
But for health, which cannot be bought or sold
  Good Manitou, fill up the glasses!

These sparkling goblets we drain to thee,
  Pike's Peak with thy beverage truthful,
And pray that thy Manitou ever may be
  The healthy, the lovely, the youthful.

ON PIKE'S PEAK.

[July 20th, 1882.]

High on the summit of Pike's Peak
  Irresolute I stand,
The clouds about me, cold and bleak
  I could touch with my hand.

The lightnings flash, the thunders crash,
  Far down beneath my feet,
And o'er the Peak the tempests dash
  A flood of snow and sleet.

Though nearer heav'n than e'er before,
  My longings earthward go ;
This solitude, it tempts me more
  And more to life below,

Where human souls and sympathies
  Form one great kindred band—
Nature is grand, but grander is
  The heartlife of our land!

SABBATH MORN.

I love on Sabbath morn
  Through forest shade to roam,
When nature seems fresh born—
  'Tis finding God at home.

Devotion enters deep
  Then in my peaceful breast,
And all the passions sleep,
  All yearning is at rest.

Then rings within my heart
  A tone of purity,
As though I were a part
  Of nature's harmony.

24

THE SPIRIT OF NIAGARA.

Have you heard of the wonderful spirit or sprite
That haunteth Niagara falls through the night?
  It hides in its mist, but anon reappears,
  And whispers dark hints in the listening ears
Of hapless mortals who wander there
Weighed down with unbearable burdens of care.

It wields over him, who at midnight hour
Approaches the falls, irresistible power,
  And woe if he listens or ventures too near,
  For onward it lures him, he loses his fear;
It beckons him down where he suffers his fate
'Mid billows and whirlpools insatiate.

On the cataract's verge is a desolate place,
Where the wild waters dash in their terrible race,
  Deep down to their gulf; but a low stone wall
  Forms here the precipitous edge of the fall,
Where gazing down from the dizzy height
Benumbs man's senses and dims the sight.

Here, on the brink of the turbulent flood,
In the darkness of night a wanderer stood,
  Of all that made life once precious and fair,
  Cruel fate had bereft him, and gloomy despair
O'er his brooding thoughts and senses had spread,
And every hope of the future lay dead.

Spellbound he lists to the thundering fall,
To the ghastly echo's reverberate call.
  Hark! from the yawning abyss at his feet
  Strange sounds float upward: "O rest, thou art
    sweet,
Thou quenchest deep in the suffering heart
The fires of anguish, its sorrows, its smart!"

"What voice do I hear from the cataract's breast!
Ye turbulent billows, what know ye of rest?"
  "It is not the falls nor the billows that spoke,
  But I, their live spirit, my silence broke;
If earnestly craved, I can give the oppressed,
If they but dare take it, the coveted rest!"

The wanderer's heart with strange hope is alight,
From the deep arise spirit-forms misty and white,
  They beckon him onward with gesture and call;
  Still closer he steps to the low-lying wall;
Imploring for mercy with arms lifted high,
He gazes at them and the cold starry sky.

He recklessly leaps on the edge of the stone,
Outstretches his hands—ah, is he not alone—
    Wife and child in the dimly-seen forms he espies,
    And then a thick darkness falls over his eyes,
He plunges beneath the all-covering wave,
And finds in the cataract's torrent his grave.

"Weak mortal!" the spirit-voice scornfully cries,
"In the battle of life thou hast missed the prize.
    For he who attempts to forestall his fate
    Shall surely be barred from the Heavenly gate.
From thy harboring faith once fallen away,
Thou becamest my victim and easy prey!"

EDELWEISS.

[Written in a Southern Cotton-field.]

On Alpine summits grows a flower,
    Of blossom tender, soft and white,
'Mid snow and ice, by cliffs surrounded,
    It proudly dwells on highest height.

The Alpine hunter seeks it boldly,
   And brings it down from heights above
The clouds, and bears it as a token
   To her to whom he gives his love.

'Tis thus not strange that of her beauty,
   High praises many a poet sang,
Whose song, by favoring zephyrs wafted,
   Like echoes o'er the ocean rang.

On shore, a little plant maturing
   Its seed, o'erheard the melody,
And spoke in accents mild and modest:
   Why cannot I thus favored be?

'Tis true, I'm not the envied token
   Of love and prowess, choice and rare,
Yet, if in patience man attends me,
   I gratefully reward his care.

The gift I hold in rough enclosure
   Is tender, soft and white as snow;
'Tis spun and woven into garments
   And worn by men where e'er they go.

A mocking bird, by chance o'erhearing
   These whispered words, sang out: How nice
And good thou art, I'll be thy poet,
   America's own Edelweiss.

Thou and the favored Alpine blossom,
  Ye both in nature fill your place;
She the ideal, thou the useful,
  Both benefit the human race.

Take—now I speak for both your nations—
  The judgment of my mocking muse:
Ideal is the Swiss; Columbia
  More practical, appreciates use.

'NEATH SOUTHERN PINES.

Wearily the slender pines o'erhang the arid ashen
    sand,
Wearily with drooping moss they try to shade the
    parching land,
Wearily with languid motion, fans the crane the
    heavy air,
Wearily from cloudless sky the sun looks down
    with steady stare;
Wearily my soul cries out: "Oh, shall life's jour-
    ney never end?"
Wearily the sleepy echo answers: "Never—ever—
    end!"

But a voice within me whispers: "Care not for
the echo's sound,
All things mortal come and perish, as the world
goes 'round and 'round.

"Time will come when all these pines no longer
shall o'erhang the land,
Time will come when all this moss will moulder
'neath the ashen sand,
Time will come when cranes no longer languidly
shall fan this air,
Time will come when thou shalt not feel weary at
the sun's bright stare,
Time will come which separates from mortal coil
the immortal soul,
Time will come when, thus set free, the latter may
approach the goal;
For, like pine, and moss, and crane, the mortal
body shall decay,
While the soul to sunny heights in lofty flight will
find its way."

THE GARDEN OF THE HESPERIDES.

A FLORIDA JEST.

"With favoring winds o'er sunlit seas
We sailed for the Hesperides"—
　As did not many years ago
　Our dear old poet "Longfellow."
That land was then but little known,
And on the seaman's charts not shown;
　Thus, leaving Massachusetts Bay,
　He steered north-east and lost his way.
And thus he found—excuse a smile—
"Ultima Thule—utmost isle,"
　Good Harriet Beecher, surnamed Stowe,
　Found, where some golden apples grow,
And, after writing "Uncle Tom,"
Sought in the sunny south a home,
　And told in book and magazine,
　What, on St. John stream may be seen.
The Hesperides—let it be stated—
E'en she had not yet penetrated.
　Let me, kind reader, therefore teach,
　Just how that garden-spot to reach:
On leaving busy Jacksonville,
Up the St. John thou travelest still.

One hundred sixty miles or more,
And landest on the eastern shore.
Here, from the city of DeLand,
Fine 'Bus and baggage-wagon stand.
  "Jump in, boss, ride with me five miles,"
  Cries jolly Jehu, full of smiles.
Palmetto and pine roots, dust and sand
Cost nothing extra in this land,
  So take them bravely, do not chide;
  It is a glorious five mile ride
Through flat woods first, then rolling pine,
Then clearings, then the land divine;
  For here the enraptured tourist sees
  The garden of the Hesperides ;
'Round house and barn, 'neath towering pine,
Millions of golden apples shine—
  Radiant reflections, as it seems,
  Of the autumn sun's most brilliant beams.
Here fanned by gentle ocean breezes,
The air is cool but never freezes— —
  Enough to hurt the orange tree;
  From killing frosts DeLand is free.
Amid its groves the wayworn guest
Is with good boarding houses blest,
  And having come o'er land and seas
  To find the famed Hesperides,
Here may he, having found the goal,
Rest easy in body, mind and soul.

LUCRETIA MOTT.

We hear the sad and melancholy bell,
  That calls the weary wanderer to her grave;
With tearful eyes we bid our last farewell
  To her, whose heart was noble, pure and brave.

The lowly and the poor throughout the land
  In her their kindest friend are called to mourn;
With sympathizing heart and helping hand
  She met the sick, the suffering and forlorn.

Among the first—to break the bondman's chains,
  Among the first—her sex to elevate,
She shunned no sacrifice, no work, no pains,
  But boldly struggled 'gainst opposing fate.

The adverse forces one by one gave way,
  She saw the former slave a man and free;
Her other radiant dream, through night and day,
  She saw maturing to reality.

Her work is done; her form the earth now claims;
　Her strong yet gentle spirit now is free;
But the fulfillment of her noble aims
　Is left to us—a sacred legacy.

Toll on! thou sad, thou melancholy bell,
　And call the weary wanderer to her grave;
With tearful eyes we bid our last farewell
　To her whose heart was noble, pure and brave!

JAMES A. GARFIELD.

DIRGE.

Black crape o'erhangs in sad ornamentation
　Our houses door by door,
A mark of sorrow of a mighty nation,
　Whose chieftain is no more.

In city, town and village, what commotion:
　The church bell sadly tolls;
A wave of grief from ocean on to ocean
　Across our country rolls.

As with one impulse fifty million people
  In prayer united bend,
And at the mournful hour their hearts, though
    distant,
  His funeral attend.

No prince or king was ever mourned as deeply
  As he, the people's choice;
In love his name is spoken by his nation
  As with one single voice.

As kind in peace as he was brave in warfare,
  E'en to his dying breath,
We held him dear, and still the tie grew closer
  By his untimely death.

Thus with two other names to memory sacred,
  His name shall ever stand:
Washington—Lincoln—Garfield—be forever
  The glory of our land.

And now farewell, thou *one* we loved so dearly,
  Thou *one* among the best;
With saddened hearts to mother earth we give
    thee,
  Garfield! Sweet be thy rest!

WELCOME VETERANS.

[At the Army Reunion 1880.]

You see our city in festal array,
In brilliant and bright decoration;
You hear our eheers, prolonged and gay,
To welcome the braves of our nation.

A score of years have nearly rolled by
Since far through our country was wired
Fort Sumter's news and the urgent cry
That men for defense were required.

The response was quick: "To arms! Arise!
Our Union must be defended!"
And into one army without much choice
The brave volunteers were blended.

Four terrible years continued the war
With frequently varying chances,
But at last on our flag shone Victory's star
Through hard-fought and bloody advances.

After many a year you meet here to-day,
Old comrades in happy reunion,
Remembering adventures both sad and gay
To recount in pleasant communion.

36

Ye veterans, once our defense and shield,
  Accept our heartiest greeting—
While for those who fell on the battle-field
  Our hearts are in sorrow still beating.

Aye, welcome once more! See the joyful throngs
  That meet here in happy communion,
To tell old tales and to sing the old songs,
  That were heard in the War for the Union!

AN ALBUM LEAF.

A wild flower grows by the murmuring brook,
  It needs neither care nor protection,
As water and air and a quiet nook
  Produce it in all its perfection.

It seems that the sky has its own bright blue
  To this beautiful favorite given;
And at night the stars show the same rich hue,
  As they bloom in the meadows of heaven.

And where in this changeable world you may be,
  If the stars that twinkle above you,
Or this flower, which grows by the brook, you
    should see,
  Remember the dear ones that love you!

CONTENTMENT.

Through North and South, through East and
    West
  We may forever roam,
If not with true contentment blest,
  We nowhere feel at home.

But if we see, where e'er we be, .
  Life's brighter, better side,
Go we or come, it seems like home,
  Wherever we abide.

POEMS

TRANSLATED.

DEDICATION.

Can'st thou not oft through leisure hours
Gaze at the face of cheery flowers,
List to the brook 'neath shady trees,
And to the humming of busy bees,
In the grass recline, and with listless gaze
Enjoy the autumn sky's blue haze;
Feel'st thou not ecstasy supreme
At spring's fresh bloom in colors bright,
Can'st longingly not rove and dream,
Bathed in the pale moon's magic light;
Art thou not thrilled with bliss divine,
When lovely eyes gaze into thine;
In short, if not a queerish wight,
Thou should'st not read the songs I write!

THE BUSY ELVES.

"O, what has become of the beautiful flowers,
  That filled so luxuriantly garden and wold?"
They were carried away by the fairies who wear
    them
  Like helmets of steel and of silver and gold.

"But where are the grassblades, that grew in the
    meadow,
  And waved in the breezes so easy and gay?"—
The elves took them also away, for they wear
    them
  As swords and as lances in battle array.

"And whither, O, whither, have all the sweet bees
    gone,
  The bees, that were busy from morning till
    night?"—
The elves and the fairies have caught them and
    ride them,
  Astride on their backs, in their aerial flight.

"What fate befell the rose, the lovely,
  With thousand leaves of blushing hue,
A golden crown within its chalice,
  And filled brim full with crystal dew?"

The fairies and elves have been sipping those dew-
    drops,
For drinking cups quickly the leaflets they chose;
The King of the elves on his head now is wearing
In splendor and glory the crown of the rose.

"But tell! have the butterflies also departed?"
  When losing the rose, Ah!—they perish forlorn;
The elves have now taken their handsome ap-
    parel,
  And use it their ladies at fetes to adorn.

"But where are the crickets, the musical fellows
  Contentedly chirping from springtime till fall?"
The elves have engaged them to sing and to fiddle
And furnish the music at every ball.

  The stately lillies, too, have vanished,
    Which grew and bloomed in tall array:
  The busy elves, with great exertion
    At last have carried them away.

They stand in their palace as beautiful columns,
   Admired at the state balls by every guest,
While high overhead on the crowns of their blos-
      soms,
   The arches of crystalline purity rest.

Now let us go home, for the valley is darkening,
   We cannot depend on the firefly's light;
They soar in the halls of the elves and are vieing
   With glittering gems in illuming the night.

The elves now rejoice in the spoils they have taken;
   O hark, how they cheer in their fastnesses deep;
And yet, they will surely restore all the treasures
   When nature awakes from her wintery sleep.

O LOVE, WHILE LOVE YOU MAY!

O love, O love, while love you may,
O love while one to love you have,
There comes an hour, the saddest hour,
When you'll be weeping at the grave!

Take care, that true your heart may be
And love require, and love inspire,
As long as in another heart
There glows for you love's radiant fire!

And he, who ope's his heart to you
O love him well—for life is brief,
And cause him all the joy you can,
And cause him not one moment's grief!

And guard your tongue, aye, guard it well;
Too soon an angry word is said,
And though the intention is not ill,
A chill comes in affection's stead!

O love, O love, while love you may,
O love while one to love you have,
There comes an hour, the saddest hour,
When you'll be weeping at the grave!

Then by the tombstone you will kneel!
And hide your eyes, with weeping dim,
Deep in the long moist graveyard grass,—
But ne'er again will they see him!—

You'll pray: "Look kindly down on me
Who at your grave is weeping still,
Forgive my rash, offensive words,
God knows I never meant them ill!"

He does not see you, does not hear
Your fervent prayer at his grave.
The lips which oft have kissed you, speak
No more: "I long ago forgave!"

He did forgive, aye, long ago,
Yet many a fervent tear did fall
For you and for your hasty words,—
But hush—he rests—he has reached the goal!

O love, O love, while love you may,
O love, while one to love you have,
There comes an hour, the saddest hour
When you'll be weeping at the grave!

A CHANGE OF HEART.

When poetry, that favored child of Heaven,
  Was born, and to the mortal world took flight,
A poet's heart was as a dwelling given
  To her, who had come down from regions bright.

She found the abode a place of strife and passion,
  Of sorrow oft, and oft of wild carouse,
So that her spirit, reared in milder fashion,
  Ere long grew weary of this haunted house.

The disappointment quite benumbed her power,
  Yet she took courage quickly to depart,
And stealthily slipped, in a happy hour,
  Into a lovely woman's tender heart.

Now if the poet wants, for happy omen,
  To see the guest whom his heart held before,
He has to rap, rap at the heart of woman,
  And whisper gently: "Please unbar the door."

FAREWELL!

We sat by the sea observing
  The waves as they rose and fell.
And they seemed to say to each other:
  We shall meet again—farewell!

And none of them stayed but a moment;
  And of all the thousands not one
Filled the place of the other, nor seemed it
  Just like the one that had gone.

Thus, coming and going, we mortals
  Press many a hand as we part:
And often the eye becomes tearful
  Whose beaming had warmed our heart.

Alas! as vanish these billows,
  Thus vanish we too without trace,
And all: joy, sorrow or sadness,
  One moment will quickly efface.

Let's bear then, through bliss and misfortune,
  Our fate as well as we may,
For our lives, like the billows before us,
  Are steadily ebbing away.

YOSEMITE.

Some Indian legends to a dale alluded,
  That nestles in a mountain range, surrounded
By lofty cliffs, from worldly strife secluded,
  And which in wondrous scenery abounded;
While on its richly irrigated sod
The form and color-giving hand of God
Beneath an azure sky bestowed its blessing;
The valley in enchanting garments dressing.

And like a passionately strong emotion
  Came the desire to see it and I turned
My steps away from the Pacific Ocean
  Back towards the East, and soon thy heights
    discerned,
Sierra Nevada! and I now ascend
Where San Joaquin's drear, desert hillocks blend
With glittering granite boulders vast and hoary,
Yet gorgeously arrayed in springtime's glory,

The air, which from the snowy peaks descended,
   Swept o'er my heated path with cooling vapors.
High ranked the sighing pines with tops extended
   Up towards the sky and straight as altar-tapers.
The mountain-torrent filled its rocky bed
And cast its spray up to the horse's head,
As on he walked, the cooling drops not heeding
O'er paths, which are 'round dread abysses leading.

And ever wilder now the scene is growing,
   And 'round me granite giants seem to rally;
Between them in the radiant sunlight showing
   Yosemite, that grand and lovely valley.
I stand amazed; the bold cliffs, huge and rude,
O'erwhelm the senses by their magnitude,
And from their edges, glittering, appaliing
With thunder sound the cataracts are falling.

The charms increase, as over rocks we enter
   Yosemite; the impetuous Merced washes
The boulders, scattered through the valley's center,
   Around and over which it swiftly dashes.
And through the atmosphere, serene and calm,
Gigantic pines exhale a fragrant balm;
So tall are they, that on the flow'ry meadow
They cast o'er oak and cedar shades their
    shadow.

Up to the sky colossal boulders tower
  Like giant domes, like monsters of past ages
Here petrified by Time's insidious power;
  Yet in whose veins seems life, for 'tween the
      ledges
Grow trees and shrubs; and many a wild-flower
      bright
Looks with its lovely face up towards the light;
Among them strange half-hidden rocks resemble
Titanic human shapes, which make one tremble.

Yosemite by one charm seems surrounded;
  Its ancient rocky fragments seem to cover
The records of a race, which once abounded
    Throughout its precincts, and whose shades still
      hover
Among the groves; and as I contemplate
This rocky valley, which until of late
Had sheltered Indian tribes, who at the nearing
Of pale-faced men were swiftly disappearing,

It calls to mind the Orient, old and distant,
  To which the gems of wisdom can be traced—
E'en as our coal we take from groves existant
  In former days, now covered and effaced—
And where the people, once in culture great,
Degenerated, and now share the fate

Of these wild Indians, who to us are bearing
But ancient tales of love and hate and daring.

The Indians die; their legendary glory
  Becomes tradition to the conquering nation,
And bears fresh fruit in poem, song and story
  From generation on to generation.
And e'en to me the new world's legend-field
Some exquisite and fragrant flowers did yield,
Which to entwine in memory's wreath I tarried,
And gladly with me to the old world carried.

IN THE FAR WEST.

In the far West I saw a country
With older nations' offsprings filling
Who, to a new life resurrected
The new world's virgin soil were tilling.
Old races, here rejuvenated,
Are into one great nation blending,
With giant strides by friendly contest,
All speedily toward progress tending.
What the coercive power of Europe
Could not achieve in ages past,
Quickly on pathways self-created
This nation, free, has gained at last.

SLANDER.

More misery than the tempest with its roaring,
  Which openly and loudly plays its part,
Is caused by sneaking slander, which is pouring
  Its poisons through the ear into the heart.

With ease the weakest points of good men finding,
  Distrust awaking, killing all belief
In truth, the eyes of love and friendship blinding,
  The slanderer is more harmful than the thief.

The robber has to risk his life when stealing;
  The slanderer ever plays a coward's game
In all he does, no higher aim revealing,
  Than to despoil men of their honest name.

AFTER THE STORM.

The rumblihg rolling of thunder,
  The flaming flashes of light
Succeeds, in beauty and wonder,
  Blissful the stillness of night.

The storm, that restless giant,
  Has fled with sullen mien,
A vanquished, yet defiant
  Rebel, before his queen.

The firmament swims glowing
  Deep in the placid stream,
Its seal of stars there showing
  Impressed in twilight gleam.

On the horizon beaming
  Spasmodic flashes leap,   .
As oft the mind, while dreaming,
  Will stir in peaceful sleep.

VINETA.

From the sea's abyss comes softly stealing
  Chimes of ev'ning bells subdued and slow,
Wondrously to those above revealing
  That old wondertown, which lies below;
Sunken lie beneath the restless ocean,
  Now its ruins buried in the deep;
From its battlements with ceaseless motion,
  Golden sparklets to the surface leap;
If the sailor sees the magic gleaming
  In the splendor of the sunset sky,
He will ever seek it, idly dreaming,
  Though surrounding it the dark cliffs lie.

From my bosom's depth come softly stealing,
  Like a chime of bells subdued and low,
Recollections, and a strange revealing
  Of the love that dwelt there long ago;
Sunken lies a lovely world there hidden,
  But its ruin, deep within my heart,
Often sends celestial sparks unbidden,
  Which in visions to the surface dart;
Then in that abyss I fain would plunge me,
  Through the leaping sparks sink deeply down,
For I feel as though the angels called me,
  Called me to the fair old wondertown.

55

TRANSITORY.

See'st thou thy shadow vanish
  Silently from the wall;
See'st thou the cloud disappearing,
  E'en while its raindrops fall;
See'st thou, rising and blending
  With air, the smoke of thine hearth?
Thus is the beginning and ending
  Of thine own life on earth!

I'M WALKING HOME.

I'm walking home from dance and pleasure,
  And take with me
Of inward sadness fullest measure, ·
  But none of glee.

I hear the dismal croak of ravens;
  With noiseless fall
The snow comes from the darksome heavens
  And covers all.

In thy descent and listless flurry,
  Thou silent snow,
O wouldst my head, my life thou bury
  And all my woe!

THE BRAVE MAN'S SONG.

High sounds the song, the brave man's song,
 Like tolling bells and organ tone;
The noble heart in danger strong,
 No gold rewards, but song alone.
Thank God, I am able my voice to raise
In singing and sounding the brave man's praise.

A moaning gale the thaw-wind blew
 From Southern seas o'er Alpine rocks;
The heavy clouds before it flew,
 As when a wolf pursues the flocks.
It shattered the forest with mighty stroke;
On lakes and on rivers the ice it broke.

On mountain summits thawed the snow;
 The fall of thousand waters roared,
Which with unbounded overflow
 Into the stream their torrents poured.
High rolled the vast waves with a costant rise,
And rolled in their current huge blocks of ice.

On pillars and on arches good,
 Of massive rock, built broad and tall,
There stretched a bridge across the flood,
 Surmounted by a cabin small.
The tollman dwelt here, with child and wife—
O, tollman ! O, tollman! quick, save thy life!

With rumbling sound the tempest rang;
  Wild raging waves the cabin shook,
When up the roof the keeper sprang,
  Upon the tempest's work to look;
"O merciful Heaven! I pray to thee!
I perish! I perish! Who rescues me?"

The ice rolled onward, crash on crash,
  And here and there from either shore,
The river, in its headlong dash,
  The pillars and the arches tore.
The terrified tollman, with wife and child,
Outshrieked in his anguish the tempest wild.

The ice rolled onward shock on shock,
  And here and there, at either end,
It battered down the blocks of rock,
  As pillar after pillar went.
Around the whole structure there yawned the
    grave—
O merciful Heaven! Have mercy, save!

High on the bank, on either side,
  A crowd of listless gazers stood;
They wrung their hands and wept and cried,
  But no one dared to brave the flood.
The terrified tollman, with wife and child,
Shrieked loudly for help through the tempest wild.

When wilt thou sound, my brave man's song,
  Like organ tone and tolling bell?
His name—withhold his name not long,
  My noblest song—when wilt thou tell?
Destruction approaches the central pier,
O brave man! O brave man! O haste, appear!

Swift galloped forth upon the strand
  A noble Count on charger bold,
What held the Count up in his hand?
  It was a purse well filled with gold;
"Two hundred pistoles I'll give to the brave
Who ventures to rescue yon three from the grave."

Who is the brave man? Wouldst thou say
  "The Count," my song? Aye, brave was he,
And good, by Heaven, he was! But stay—
  My hero must still braver be!
O braver man! Braver man! Haste, appear!
Advancing perdition is drawing near!

The flood dashed higher on the bank,
  And louder roared and shrieked the blast:
And deeper still the courage sank!
  O Saver! Saver! Come at last!
Still pillar on pillar was doomed to fall:
Loud crashed into ruin the arches all.

"Halloo! Halloo! Cheer up and dare!"
  Thus cried the noble Count aloud.
They heard his words, but none did care
  To risk his life, of all that crowd.
In vain did the tollman, with wife and child,
  Cry loudly for help through the tempest wild.

There, staff in hand, a husbandman
  With steady step came walking by;
His garb was homespun, coarse and plain,
  His face was kind, his stature high.
He stopped when he heard what the Count had
      said,
And gazed at the threatening abyss ahead.

And then, his trust in God, he dashed
  Into a skiff, that had been beached,
And, spite the ice, which 'round him crashed,
  The central pier he safely reached.
But woe! The boat was too small, too small,
In one bold effort to save them all.

Thus three times pushed he off the strand
  In spite of whirlpool, storm and wave;
And three times was he seen to land,
  Till all were rescued from the grave;
For scarce had he landed the last on shore,
When pillar and cabin fell toppling o'er.

Who is, who is, the man so brave?
  My song, O let his name be told!—
The peasant risked his life to save;
  Perhaps he did it but for gold?
Perchance, if the Count had not offered his meed,
That man had not ventured his life in the deed.

"Here," cried the Count, "my valient friend,
  Is the reward thou well hast won!"
In truth, we must the Count commend,
  Forsooth, Sir Count, 'twas nobly done!—
But higher, aye, holier throbbed indeed
The heart that the peasant's coarse garment hid.

"For gold my life was not at stake,
  Though I am poor, I hunger not,
The tollman may thy bounty take,
  He lost his all in yonder flood!"
Thus answered the peasant in accents kind,
And, walking away, left the crowd behind.

High sound my song, my brave man's song,
  Like tolling bells and organ tone!
That noble heart, in danger strong,
  No gold rewards, but song alone.
Thank God! I am able my voice to raise,
To render immortal that hero's praise!

FAITH.

Let winter freeze, let winter blow,
   Through glade and forest roaming,
And cover them with ice and snow—
   Yet spring, bright spring, is coming.

Let ugly fogs o'ercast the Sun—
   My faith shall not be shaken—
He will from up on His high throne
   The earth to joy awaken.

Blow on, ye storms, with all your might,
   Your power I am not fearing;
With noiseless footsteps over night,
   Bright spring shall be appearing.

Then shall the earth in buoyant bliss
   Awaken and silently wonder,
And smile at the Sun and his heavenly kiss,
   And look at him sweeter and fonder.

Bright blooming wreaths she will weave
    'round her brow
Of many a beautiful flower.
Her springs, like tears of joy, will flow,
   With most irresistible power.

Fear not, though from thy heart the chill
　Thy blood has almost driven—
A grand and glorious May-day will
　Yet to the world be given.

And when into this life almost
　Hell seems to have ascended;
Be strong, my soul—in God thy trust—
　All anguish shall be ended!

HOPE.

As the waves on waves are broken
　Yet the sea is not undone;
Hope on hope is disappointed,
　Yet the heart hopes on and on.

As the rise and fall of billows
　Constitute the ocean's life;
Thus the living heart forever
　Is with hopeful fancies rife.

As the ocean's waving summits
　Spray o'er spray toward heaven send;
Thus from deep within our bosoms
　Hope's fond dreams will e'er ascend.

TO MY MOTHER.

It is my way to hold my head erect;
My mind and will are rather strong and stern,
And e'en the king's own glances could not turn
My eyelids down, his pride I could reject.

But thine eyes, mother dear, at once correct
The pride and anger which within me burn,
For in thy blissful presence I discern
My heart with timid humbleness deject.

Is it thy spirit's subtle conquering power,
Thy noble mind, with heavenly light transcended,
That penetrates and sees my soul so clearly;

Is it the memory of many an hour,
When thee, without intent I have offended,
Which bows me to thy heart, that loves me dearly?

NIGHT THOUGHTS.

The thought of Germany at night
Drives slumber from my pillow quite,
  My mind recalls the day of parting,
  And hot, resistless tears are starting.

The years have come, the years have passed
Since, mother dear, I saw thee last.
  Twelve years have gone—gone unreturning—
  Yet grow my longing and my yearning.

My yearning and my longing grow,
The mother has bewitched me so;
  I think of her, as of no other,
  May God preserve her, dear old mother.

The dear old dame, she loves me so!
In trembling lines her letters show,
  By signs that cannot be mistaken,
  How deeply her fond heart is shaken.

Of her I think where'er I stay;
Twelve long, long years have passed away;
  Twelve years 'mong strangers have distressed
    me
  Since to her true heart she has pressed me.

Ah, Germany lives evermore,
It is a land sound to the core,
  With oaks and lindens firmly rooted,
  Whene'er I wish, I can salute it.

For Germany I should not care
So much were not my mother there,
  For it no trouble need I borrow,
  But she I love, may die to-morrow.

Ah, since I left my native land,
Death touched with unrelenting hand
  My early friends, aye many perished,
  Whom in my youth I fondly cherished.

And if I count the shadowy crowd,
My heart in anguish throbs aloud.
  Could I those mournful figures banish,
  I should have rest. Thank God, they vanish!

Thank God! Athwart the window pane
Serene French daylight shines again;
  In comes my wife, like morn' in gladness
  And smiles away my German sadness.

A MISTAKE.

A pretty maid was walking
  Some hedgerow trees beneath,
And picking fragrant flowers
  To weave into a wreath.

As she plucked some opening roses
  With her dainty fingertips,
A butterfly alighted
  And kissed her rosy lips;

Then whispered: "Oh, beg pardon,
  I came for honey's sake,
And thought these lips were roses;
  Forgive the slight mistake!"

"This time I will forgive thee!"
  Replied the maiden shy,
"But mark: Such roses bloom for
  No naughty butterfly!"

CHAMPAGNE.

Half a million lusty devils
  Once upon this earth were thrown,
But alas for these poor devils,
  Not a penny did they own.

All were sniveling, whining, crying,
  Weeping and lamenting too,
For the poor deluded rascals
  Did not know what they should do.

Satan, the old chief of devils,
  Laughed till he would almost split:
"Gracious heavens, these poor devils
  Are without a grain of wit!"

And they scratched their ears in wonder,
  Bordering almost on despair:
"We are lost, we are, by thunder,
  'Tis a horrible affair!"

Then spoke Weeweefax, the small one,
  "Ye are dull as empty straw,
I alone am of ye all one
  Only devil *comme il faut!*

"Ye have thirst and naught to quench it,
  Suffering thus infernal pain.
There's a goblet, let us clench it
  Fast, and all is well again!

"See that wine vault window's blinking,
  Quick our quarters there we'll take,
And, into its deep hold sinking,
  Many a bottle's cork seal break!

"Though the doors are barricaded
  With big bolts we can't unloose,
We can glibly glide unaided
  Through the keyhole if we choose."

"Hie!" they yelled through parching throttles,
  Slipping down in steadfast line,
Emptying half a million bottles
  Of the best and oldest wine.

And they sang in mirthful chorus,
  Gaily guzzling all that night,
"What excells the wine before us?
  That and love makes all things bright!"

When toward morn the cocks were crowing
  The imps at empty bottles sneered,
Most hilarious faces showing—
  Satan suddenly appeared.

Forced into these empty bottles,
   All these devils full of ire,
Pressing corks into the throttles,
   Tied them down with toughest wire.

Half a million drunken devils
   In these bottles seem at rest;
By consent the mortals call them,
   "Dry champagne, of wines the best!"

When the corks are gaily popping,
   Out they slip, quite fresh and gay,
Vent their mirth beyond all stopping—
   Then the devil is to pay.

ST. MARY'S CRADLE SONG.

Angels that soft
   'Neath palm trees are flying,
Guard that aloft
   All the winds cease their sighing,
Hold down the branches,
   So that the wild
Winds will not wake him;
Sweet slumbers my child.

Palm trees of Bethlehem,
  How ye are roaring!
Is the mad tempest
  Over you soaring?
Gale, change to whispers
  Thy loud voice, not wild
Rush through the tree-tops,
  Sweet slumbers my child.

Ah, for sweet slumber's
  Wonderful blessing,
Yearned the tired child
  I am caressing.
Earthly cares easy
  By dreams are beguiled;
Hush, oh ye tree-tops,
  Sweet slumbers my child.

Dampness and chill air
  About the boy hover;
What can I do
  Him more warmly to cover?
Oh, guardian angels!
  Descend soft and mild,
Hold down the branches—
  Let slumber my child!

THE CAPTIVE.

Don Francisco in the dungeon
  Sat, deep woe his form had bent;
Lonely mourned his dear old mother
  O'er her son's imprisonment.

A guitar she kindly offered
  As a present to her son:
"Sing a song and let thy fingers
  Sound the four strings' richest tone!"

"Ah, how can I sing, dear mother,
  In the prison's dismal night?"
"Grief before thy song will vanish,
  Just as darkness shuns the light!"

Don Francisco sings—mute listens
  To his song the nightingale;
Gentler runs the brook's mild current,
  Hushed and charmed, as in a spell.

And the song's sweet tones are reaching
  E'en the queen's high balcony;
And her page forgets his duty,
  Goes, the singer to espy.

But the queen is promenading
  On the castle's highest part,
Asks, "Who is the lovely singer,
  That can charm the ear and heart?"

"He who sings is Don Francisco,
  In the dungeon, dark and lone!"
Quickly spoke the queen: "Oh, happy
  She, who calls that singer son!"

Quickly spoke the young Infanta:
  "Give him as mine own to me!"
Quickly, too, the page departed
  Then, to set the singer free.

Don Francisco kissed his shackles,
  Raised in prayer his hands above,
"Praised be chain and pain and prison,
  Where I found both song and love!"

THE ROCK OF STEPHAN.*

A giant rock stands by the Volga,
  With clinging moss clad o'er and o'er;
Through ages it has stood and guarded
  In changeless might, the river's shore.

High heaven's free winds blow, never weary
  About its bare and hoary peak;
The mighty eagle plucks upon it
  His bleeding game with cruel beak.

No mortal ever scaled its summit,
  Except one hero known to fame;
For whom that rock has ever after
  In grateful fancy borne his name.

To be alone for contemplation
  He scaled its pinnacle one night,
And 'mid the stillness sat and pondered
  Until the early morning light.

---

*Stephan Razin was the leader of the great insurrection of serfs in Russia in the seventeenth century; but after nearly three years of hard fighting, and almost superhuman exertions on his part, he was captured and tortured to death in Moscow. His memory still lives among the poorer classes of Russia, and the above ballad, published by the "Underground press," created great sensation in that country.

Grand glorious thoughts in his lone anguish
  Were born that night within his soul;
He formed, high o'er the murmuring river
  A plan to reach a noble goal.

And full of gloom, yet firm in purpose,
  He left the rock at sunrise hour,
Determined for the cause of freedom
  To shake the czar's imperial power.

But force and fate combined against him,
  His daring deeds were all in vain;
Though streams of blood were shed in battle,
  The serf did not his freedom gain.

He entered Moscow—not on horseback,
  Nor as a war-chief, in command
Of conquering hosts—he came a captive
  And perished by the hangman's hand.

Thus died Stephan Razin not telling
  His inmost thoughts to living man,
But to that rock alone he whispered
  In dark of night his deep-laid plan.

The rock still stands in gloomy glory,
  And guards those thoughts and Volga's shore.
It's name reminds the Russian peasants
  Of their brave chief, who is no more.

Ah! if there be a man in Russia
  Who is too good to oppress a slave,
Loves freedom as he loves his mother,
  Is wise in peace, in battle brave,

Let him ascend that rock at midnight,
  Press on its crest his watchful ear;
He can unseal the mighty secret—
  Stephan's own thoughts he then shall hear.

MISS DOCTOR FAIR.

Why needle and thread!?
There is in my head
  Sufficient phosphoric and luminous brain!
  I'll study for doctor, like many a man—
And so she did, and looked quite neat
With cap, and skirt which showed her feet.
  She carried her books tucked under her arm,
  And studied her little head quite warm.
She missed no lecture, was bright and smart;
Anatomy was her favorite part.
  With classical mien a corpse she could slice,
  And held her nose only once or twice;
Her doctor's title she well had earned,
And went to work quite unconcerned.
  From here and there and everywhere
  Came patients to "Miss Doctor Fair."
Among them came a handsome youth,
He suffered—well—to tell the truth:
  No other doctor yet could please
  This chap, he had the heart disease.
In curing him she lost her name,
And then no other patients came;
  They stayed away, nor were they wanted,
  Because her house was baby-haunted.

SONG OF THE MOON.

To thy window shining brightly,
  Come the moonlight's gentle beams,
Touching on thy curtains lightly
  Whilst thou dreamest restless dreams.

Oh, refuse me not admission,
  Me, the moon, thy friendly guest:
I can aid thy dreaming vision,
  I can give thee sweeter rest.

Sorrow, doubt and sad repining
  I have often charmed away;
Dreams I edge with silver lining,
  Give to fancy easy sway.

Never chiding or reproving
  Friends for aught I may espy,
Silently I'm onward moving
  Till Aurora lights the sky.

A COSSACK SONG.

An ivy vine in the garden crept,
  Along the earth so low;
Near by a lovely maiden wept,
  Her heart was full of woe.

"Why twinest thou, green blooming vine,
  Not upward, toward the sky?"
"Why droopest thou, O maiden fine,
  In sorrow, head and eye?"

"How can the ivy upward twine,
  Supportless and alone?
How can the maid's eyes gladly shine?—
  Her Cossack friend is gone."

THE OLD COSSACK.

O'er the Black Sea flies the eagle;
  Upward, skyward he is sweeping;
But the Cossack, old and lonely,
  O'er his youth, misspent, is weeping.

Cries: "O years of youth and manhood,
  Whither have ye all been banished?
Have ye in the fields and meadows,
  Have ye in the green woods vanished?"

What but yesterday the Cossack
  Gained, from danger never shrinking,
Brings no blessing, for he spends it
  Listlessly to-day in drinking!

THE BROOK.

Oh tell me, brook, whose course runs free through
    meadows, groves and fields,
Thou, whose clear flood to all of them such pure
    refreshment yields,
Why is thy current's melody with doleful tones so
    rife,
Although of all things known to me thine seems
    the gayest life?

The brook replied: "Of earthly bliss there's
    naught belongs to me;
By fate's decree I'm doomed to roam and hasten
    toward the sea;
The rose may bloom, the laurel twine, and seem
    prepared to meet me,
The slender willow and the vine wait on the shore
    to greet me;
There would be bliss to tarry then, but not a mo-
    ment's stay
Will fate allow.—I longingly look up and haste
    away!"

In silence then the brook ran on while I stood on
    the shore;
Tears filled my eyes and, ah, my heart was sad-
    dened to the core;
Possession of my inmost soul the dark reflection
    took,
That human life on earth is like that never resting
    brook!

EPIGRAMS OF OMAR KHAYYAM.

THE PERSIAN.

A potter near his modest cot
Was shaping many an urn and pot;
He took the clay for the earthen things
From beggar's feet and heads of kings.

———

Know ye why the Cypress tree as freedom's tree is
　known?
Know ye why the Lily fair as freedom's flower is
　shown?
Hundred arms the Cypress has, yet never plunder
　seeks;
With ten well-developed tongues, the Lily never
　speaks!

———

With mine own heart I am in constant strife,
　　　What shall I do?
Remembrance of past errors blights my life,
　　　What shall I do?
Though kindly Thou, O Lord, my sins forgivest,
Their mem'ry still within my heart is rife,
　　　What shall I do?

Like wind flies Time 'tween birth and death;
Therefore, as long as thou hast breath,
Of care for two days hold thee free;
The day that was and is to be.

———

No fear have I of life nor death—
The dreaded flight of soul and breath;
But not to do my duty here
And die—shall be my constant fear.

———

Attempt not to fathom the secrets of heaven,
But gratefully use what to thee is here given;
For none have returned from that realm of bliss,
To tell how those fared who have prayed much in
    this.

———

I doubt whether those who through every clime
    Have wandered and sought, in peace and in strife,
For gold and for treasures, have ever found time
    To study the genuine value of life.

Many of our leading men are rotten cores in glittering shells;
Wealth, position may be theirs, but in their heart no comfort dwells;
So perverted are they oft, that only those they can respect
Who, like them, for sordid causes all the nobler aims neglect.

———

To-morrow's fate, though thou be wise,
Thou canst not tell nor yet surmise;
Pass therefore not to-day in vain,
For it will never come again.

———

The Prophet's followers seek Kaba's shrine;
Bells call the Christian hosts in prayer to join—
Cross, rosary, and pulpit will I praise,
If they but prove safe guides to Truth Divine.

———

The heart that has no power of self-denial
Severely suffers, suffers many a trial;
The unselfish heart feels bliss without alloy
In causing others happiness and joy.

The world will turn when we are earth
    As though we had not come nor gone;
There was no lack before our birth,
    When we are gone there will be none.

———

Friend! believe in dogmas only such as lift the
    soul to God;
If thy neighbor should be needy, go, alleviate his
    lot;
Shun deceit, be just and kind, and cause no fellow-
    being pain,
Then wilt thou contentment here, hereafter life
    eternal, gain.

FAITH AND UNBELIEF.

To Thee what is faith, what is unbelief, Lord!
What the quarrels of priesthood o'er sentence or
    word!
Only he knows Thee not, who his own heart not
    knows,
As wood doubts the fire till ignited it glows!
The outer world shows us but little of Thee,
Whom yet our soul's vision may readily see!
Thou art of the spirit, of life the first cause!
And what from Thee comes, ever back to Thee
    flows!
From Thee comes all truth and to Thee it returns,
While like shadow and show are all earthly con-
    cerns.
The spring feeds the sea and the sea feeds the
    spring,
Between them the rivers and clouds form the ring.
Thou partest, unitest with ordering hand
The earth and the heaven, and water and land!
To Thee 'tis the same, suns or flowers to create,
And nothing is small to Thee, nothing is great!
Thou countest not present, nor future nor past,
Wast all at beginning, wilt all be at last!
The works of all men, be they wicked or kind,
Disappear before Thee e'en as chaff in the wind!
While to keen understanding oft hidden thou art,
Thou revealest Thyself to the true, loving heart!